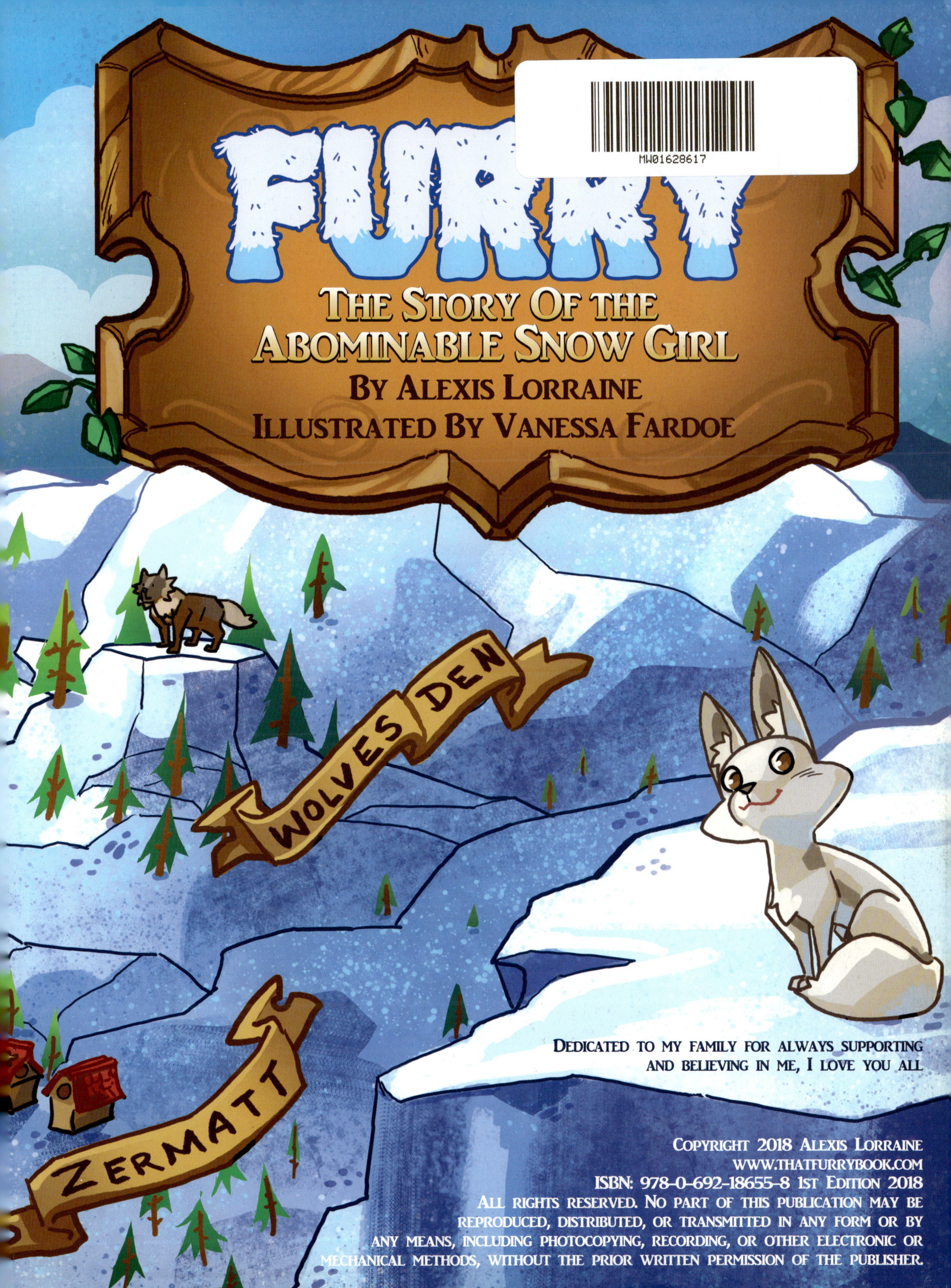

Dedicated to my family for always supporting
and believing in me, I love you all

www.thatfurrybook.com
ISBN: 978-0-692-18655-8 1st Edition 2018

Once upon a time, there stood a kingdom below the snow capped majesty of Matterhorn Mountain. Zermatt was a very rich kingdom that thrived from the hard work of the townspeople, who mined the Matterhorn for it's precious gems and minerals.

They built an extensive cave system within the mountain to go in and out, using bobsleds to bring their bounty down to the kingdom below.

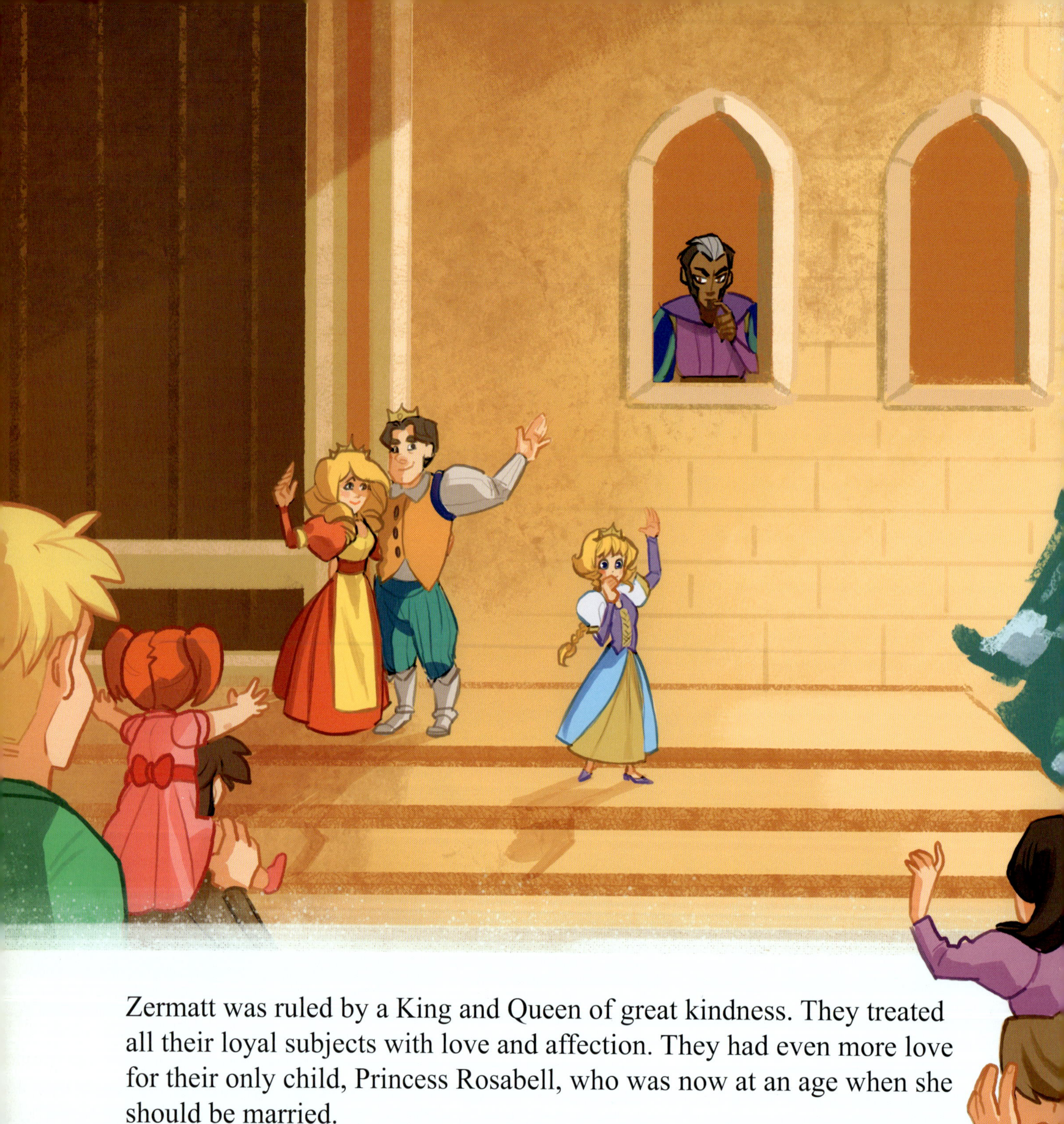

Zermatt was ruled by a King and Queen of great kindness. They treated all their loyal subjects with love and affection. They had even more love for their only child, Princess Rosabell, who was now at an age when she should be married.

The kingdom was brought luck by the Young Wizard, Liborio, whom the King and Queen loved like a son of their own. They had taken the magical boy in when he was just a child, his father having disappeared on a quest up the Matterhorn. Growing up with Princess Rosabell, he fell madly in love with her, but was always too shy to profess his love.

The King and Queen saw Liborio as a perfect match for their daughter, already considering him part of the family. A marriage between him and Rosabell would only strengthen the kingdom. Much to his delight, they declared that Rosabell would be married to Liborio.

Princess Rosabell, however, had no intention of marrying the young wizard. Her heart belonged to another, Franco, a young man in town whom she had fallen deeply in love with. Franco, the lowly apprentice of the local blacksmith, would never be considered a suitable husband for Princess Rosabell. Unlike Rosabell, Franco wasn't born into royalty. He worked hard all his life. She loved this about him.

As the wedding day neared, Rosabell knew she had to marry Franco before it was too late. Her love for him had grown so great that she could not turn back. She would not be married to another.

That night Rosabell and Franco snuck away to be married in secret, by a young priest who believed love could never be forced.

On his way to visit his future bride and talk of the wedding plans, Liborio saw Rosabell sneak away with Franco. Not knowing what to think, he followed them.

When he witnessed their vows, his heart broke sending him into a furious rage. How could she do this to him? She was his one true love. She didn't deserve to be loved by anyone else, ever again.

What kind of monster would do such a thing as to break the heart of the one who loved her the most!

Princess Rosabell and Franco crept quietly back into the castle, where they would spend their first night as husband and wife. Liborio's anger had overcome any sense of good he had left inside, which caused him to cast a spell on the newlyweds:

“This ugly deed will bring upon ugly results, your love is meant only for the monsters that you are, and the love of monsters will be all that you ever know!”

The two were transformed into creatures the world had never seen before. They both became covered in fur and their faces were transformed into those of monstrous beasts. Rosabell and Franco didn’t know what to do as they stumbled around the room in their new forms.

A chamber maid heard the ruckus and went in to make sure Rosabell was okay. She was horrified to find two monsters with Princess Rosabell's clothes torn to shreds below them.

She called for the guards, who then attacked the two beasts that appeared to have eaten the princess. Rosabell and Franco escaped the castle and fled to the mountain.

Their new forms made it much easier to travel the harsh landscape of the Matterhorn. The guards gave chase, but once on the mountain they had to turn back because the conditions were too much.

The King and Queen found the shredded clothing of their once beautiful daughter and fell into a great sadness. Their hearts broke from the loss of their only child. Time passed and they started to neglect their kingdom.

The townspeople were too afraid to mine the Matterhorn, as stories grew of two creatures that lived within the tunnels. The King and the Queen soon died, as their heart break was too great. With no one to rule the kingdom, Liborio took control. Liborio grew older and his heart had nearly turned to stone. A dark time befell the once prosperous kingdom.

The once great kingdom was now nothing more than a shell of it's former self. The houses decayed, the streets barren, and many had left the kingdom in hopes of finding work elsewhere. The people of Zermatt abandoned the mines due to the fear of what lurked within.

Liborio ruled with an iron fist. He wouldn't tolerate any disobedience from his subjects, causing more to leave for fear of his wrath. The only friend he had was his trusty pet Blanko, a mischievous snow leopard. A true sadness had swept over the entire kingdom, in all but one place.

Within the tunnels of the Matterhorn, Rosabell and Franco lived with their daughter Nora, a happy family of furry monsters. There was no one like Nora aside from her parents, so she made friends with all the wonderful animals that lived on the mountain.

There was an arctic fox named Hans who may have been small in stature but felt like he was as big as a bear. Georgio the owl, whose wisdom was greater within his mind than in reality. Francie the mountain hare, who was filled with energy and always had a smile on her face showing her big buck teeth. Romeo the marmot, who may be small, but had a giant heart ready for romance. And Bruno the ibex, who had taken too many bumps to the head over the years.

They always watched over her and kept her out of trouble. Still, Nora was lonely, even with all her animal friends. There was no one that was quite like her. She would never know the love that her parents shared. As she looked out from the caves, she could see Zermatt down below. Her parents told her never to go there as the townspeople saw them only as monsters. So Nora gazed past the town of Zermatt. *Out there, there must be someone,* she thought. Someone for her.

In the neighboring kingdom of Varallo a foreign army from the east was attacking, lead by the powerful General Khan. All the men of the kingdom stood tall to battle the foreign army, including the King and all four sons. Well, all except one, Prince Marco. Prince Marco, who was thin, gangly, with eyes peering through thick-rimmed glasses, was afraid of his own shadow, let alone that of any army.

He wasn't like his brothers, who were all rugged and handsome manly men. As his father and brothers stood tall to do battle, the cowardly prince fled the city on his trusty steed Thomas. The fear of battle was too great for him, so he would flee to another town where he would be safe.

After a long ride, Prince Marco came upon Zermatt. It looked desolate and abandoned, as if no one had lived there for many years. He rode through the town wondering if it was haunted. He could see no life, but could hear scurrying about. Eventually some townspeople crept shyly from their decayed homes. Marco asked them to take him to the King and Queen. The townspeople obliged, but warned him there was no longer a king or queen, but an evil wizard.

Marco thought this to be ludicrous, an evil wizard running a kingdom? The townspeople took him to the castle and upon a simple introduction he now knew the townspeople were telling the truth. Marco presented himself as Prince Marco from Varallo and that he was traveling west and was seeking room and board in this kingdom. As Blanko smelled the fear on Marco, Liborio gladly offered him a safe stay in his kingdom for the night. He summoned for one of his servants to take Marco to his room.

Upon the discovery of the last heir to the throne having escaped his clutches, General Khan sent teams of soldiers out to the closest kingdoms, Domodossola and Zermatt. After riding all night, Khan's army reached Zermatt. Upon arrival they went straight to the castle, where they were greeted by Liborio and Blanko.

They explained they were looking for a young prince from Varallo. The foreign army offered a reward and promised to leave the kingdom alone for Liborio's help. Liborio had no ties to the young prince, so he quickly alerted the foreign army to his location within the castle. Marco had already risen from his slumber and saw the army approaching.

As the army burst through the door, he clumsily fell out the window and down the side of the building, where Thomas was waiting. He jumped on Thomas' back and rode off quickly as the army ran through the castle after him. More of the army was set up around the kingdom and quickly closed off Marco's exits.

Marco was forced up the Matterhorn. The army gave chase. The terrain was getting too rough for Thomas when they came upon a tunnel. Marco thought it was a good hiding place. He dismounted from Thomas and pushed him into the tunnel, then followed behind.

They ran deep into the tunnel, where there was no light, and sat down against a wall. He could hear the army approaching. This was going to be it, his last stand. He told Thomas not to worry, then readied himself. Sword in hand, he waited for the army to approach. He wouldn't go down without a fight.

As the torches came closer, his heart beat faster and faster. The army could see him now, and he raised his sword, for the battle was upon him. Suddenly the army shrieked, and they quickly turned around and ran out of the cave. He had done it! The army knew the power of a prince was too much for them. He swung his sword around triumphantly. Because he was clumsy and not much of a sword smith, it slipped out of his hands. As the light dimmed from the army leaving the tunnel, he couldn't see anything.

At the same time he could hear what sounded like an animal breathing. He told Thomas to relax. Thomas neighed. It wasn't him. Marco's heart started to race. What if he had stumbled into the cave of a bear? As he ran his hand across the ground looking for his sword, he felt something furry. A foot. *Oh no, it must be a bear!* Marco gulped, then remembered he had some matches in his pocket. He struck a match, which revealed a furry foot. He raised the flame higher and higher until he was face to face with Nora the Abominable snow girl. Thomas passed out upon seeing the beast, and then she spoke, "Hey that's my foot." Marco screamed in horror and quickly passed out next to his trusty steed.

Marco awoke with a smile as Bruno licked his face. He saw Georgio perched above looking down at him with disapproving eyes. He felt a lick on his finger-tips and glanced down at Francie, who smiled up at him with her big buck teeth. This put him at ease. His smile quickly faded when Nora was suddenly standing over him with Hans growling by her side. He quickly scrambled back against the wall in fear. Hans approached him, teeth snarling.

Nora said,"Oh hey, you're awake. Hans will you relax?" Hans backed away. Marco couldn't believe that this beast could speak. The animals all seemed to be talking to Nora as she looked at each one of them, telling them that they'll be fine. Nora told them they now had a new friend. Marco calmed down and realized that Nora wasn't there to hurt him. Then Thomas walked in with food in his mouth. Seeing Marco awake, Thomas smiled and ran to him. Marco hugged Thomas happy to see a familiar face.

Thomas smiled as Nora put her hand on him and ran her furry fingers through his hair. Marco was at complete ease now. This beast obviously meant him no harm. He explained that he came from a neighboring kingdom that was attacked by a foreign army led by the evil General Khan. He didn't let Nora know he was a prince. He wasn't sure who he could trust.

Nora tried to convince her animal companions that they all must band together and help their new friend Marco defeat this foreign army. Hans wanted nothing to do with this, because Marco was a human and humans couldn't be trusted. The rest of the animals appeared scared. They'd never faced humans before, especially in a battle.

Marco didn't think they would be enough. General Khan's men were fierce and wouldn't give up easily. Nora said they must go see Orso the great wise bear that lived at the top of the Matterhorn. They would have to be careful though, as the path to the top went through the land of the mountain wolves, who were the enemy tribe of all the other animals of the Matterhorn. As Nora and Marco made their way to the top, Marco was constantly hearing things and looking over his shoulder.

What if the wolves were near? Nora calmed him down and told him not to worry. She'd take care of any wolves that crossed their path. Just then, three wolf scouts jumped out from behind some rocks and surrounded Nora and Marco. They asked them what they were doing in their land. Nora told them they were just passing through and meant them no harm. The head of the scouts said they were breaking the treaty by traveling through their land without permission and must be punished. Marco didn't know what to do, so he drew his sword. This enraged the wolves, and they attacked.

Marco swung blindly as they lunged at him. Nora fought two of the wolves off as they bit her arms and pulled at her legs. Her thick fur was like armor against their sharp fangs. Marco backed up against some rocks. He was cornered. He took a big gulp and raised his sword as a wolf lunged at him. Suddenly Nora knocked the wolf to the ground, then grabbed him by the tail and swung him around. When she let go, he went flying into the other two wolves that were trying to regain their bearings after Nora had given them a good thrashing. The three wolves tumbled down the snow bank.

When they rose, Nora growled with a fierceness no wolf could match. The wolves turned tail and ran off yelping. Nora turned to Marco who was shaken from the experience, slumped down against the rocks. She offered her furry hand to him and pulled him up. Marco thanked her. Nora said it was nothing and nudged Marco on the shoulder. Her strength being so great, Marco quickly fell down. They both giggled and Nora helped Marco up again. Marco smiled at his new friend knowing he could really trust her, even with his life.

Upon reaching the top of the mountain they found the entrance to the cave of Orso the great wise bear. Orso was believed to have lived there for over a hundred years and had the answers to every question imaginable. While Nora and Marco were gone, the foreign army attacked the caves, using explosives to blow up many of the tunnels. Nora's companions were not ready to fight off this foreign army.

Rosabell and Franco, not knowing what was coming, were captured by the army when they could not find Prince Marco. Rosabell and Franco were taken back to Zermatt Castle, where the army could plan their next attack and have Liborio shed some light on these creatures that lived within the tunnels.

At the top of the mountain, Nora asked Orso what they should do about this foreign army. Orso told her they must consult the sacred ice. The ice within the cave had been there for thousands of years, and if the question you asked came from a place of truth within your heart, the ice would show you the answer. Orso raised his paws and chanted at the great ice wall. Wind and ice crystals whipped through the cave. Orso pushed Nora forward and told her to ask. Nora asked the ice what they must do.

The ice showed all the animals of the mountain, including the wolves, standing together with the foreign army at their feet. Orso told Nora and Marco they must unite all the animal tribes of Matterhorn Mountain to defeat the foreign army. Nora told Orso she wasn't sure if the wolf tribe would help them. Upon these words, the image in the ice changed, the animals separated, and an image of the caves exploding and fires burning within the snow appeared. Orso told them that if they didn't unite the animal tribes the foreign army would destroy the mountain and they all would have no home.

Upon arriving home, Nora was shocked to discover many of her animal companions injured, her parents gone, and her home nearly destroyed. Hans angrily pointed at Marco and said that it was all his fault.

After Nora calmed Hans down he told her that the foreign army came looking for Marco and they couldn't fight them off. The army had explosives that caused all the damage.

They also took her parents. Nora ran to the section of the cave where her parents usually were and found it almost completely destroyed. This made Nora very angry. She told Marco to stay there and that the army wouldn't get away with this.

Nora told Marco that she must go see the king of the mountain wolves while he stayed there. With anger in her heart, Nora set out to see the king of the mountain wolves.

While Nora was gone, Marco saw all the destruction around him. He now knew the full power of this foreign army. He slumped down against a wall and looked at the wounded animals. His heart grew sad. He never meant for any of this to happen. Hans walked up holding a small marmot in his mouth. The marmot hadn't made it through the battle. Hans dropped the marmot at Marco's feet and growled at him.

Marco realized this was all his fault. These poor animals suffered because of him. Hans looked Marco in the eyes and made a motion for him to leave. Marco was not be able to speak to Hans, but he understood. He had to leave, as he was the cause of all of this. If he was gone, the army would leave them alone.

As he packed up his things, Francie nudged him with her bandaged ear. Marco looked down at the poor little creature and exclaimed,"You can't stop me. I've already caused enough trouble here. This isn't your fight."

Marco took Thomas and left the mountain in hopes of disappearing farther west and saving his new friends from any more trouble.

Upon arriving on the other side of the Matterhorn, Nora was greeted with hostility. The wolves thought she was back for another fight. She demanded they take her to their leader, King Aldo. They obliged. King Aldo had no interest in hearing what Nora had to say, but she explained that if they didn't all unite against this army, they all could fall victim to it and their homes could be lost.

King Aldo didn't trust or like any other animals of the mountain. He pointed out how she just beat up three of his best scouts. He looked at them bandaged in the corner, looking defeated. Nora explained she meant them or him no harm, but was simply defending herself against their attack. King Aldo looked to the scouts who nodded in agreement.

After he thought it over, King Aldo agreed to form a pact with Nora to defeat this foreign army. Even he would not stand by and let anyone destroy his home.

As Marco moved west, his head hung low. He knew he'd made a mistake, but what could he do? They'd be better off without him, right? Thomas looked at him with sad eyes. He knew Marco was doing the wrong thing.

Marco looked up at a tree and saw two birds flying around, playing like the best of friends. He remembered Nora's smile as they traveled to see Orso and how she saved him in the face of danger. Marco lowered his head in shame. Was he turning his back on one of the only true friends he'd ever had?

When Nora returned with the mountain wolves, she found Marco gone. Hans told her they were better off without Marco, that the army would not pursue them once they rescued Rosabell and Franco. Marco was who they wanted. This made Nora sad, but she wouldn't let it deter them from protecting their home.

Nora devised a battle plan with King Aldo to rescue her parents and defeat the foreign army. She didn't need Marco. She had her animal companions who had always been there for her.

All the animals were banded together now, ready to attack Zermatt Castle. They descended and a great battle ensued. Georgio and the owls dropped rocks on the soldiers helmets. Bruno and the other ibex rammed the soldier's shields, knocking them back while Romeo and his pals grabbed their heels and knocked them to the ground. The wolves pounced on the soldiers, snarling and ripping at their clothes.

A few soldiers closed in on Nora as she protected Francie, who was too small and timid for the battle. Nora didn't know what to do. The soldiers swords were drawn. She backed up, keeping Francie behind her. She might get hurt, but no harm would come to her friend. She growled furiously as the soldiers raised their swords, ready to strike. The soldiers showed no fear, and Nora turned and covered Francie.

As the swords came swinging down, Marco arrived out of nowhere on Thomas, who bashed head first into the soldiers, knocking them to the ground. Hans quickly ran up and pulled their swords away, leaving them without weapons to fight.

Marco yelled to Nora,"Hey, you didn't think I'd let you have all the fun without me?" Nora turned from covering her friend to see Marco, as well as the soldiers on the ground. She smiled, jumped to her feet, and snarled at the weaponless soldiers, who quickly got up and ran. With the soldiers retreating, the animals and Nora rescued Rosabell and Franco.

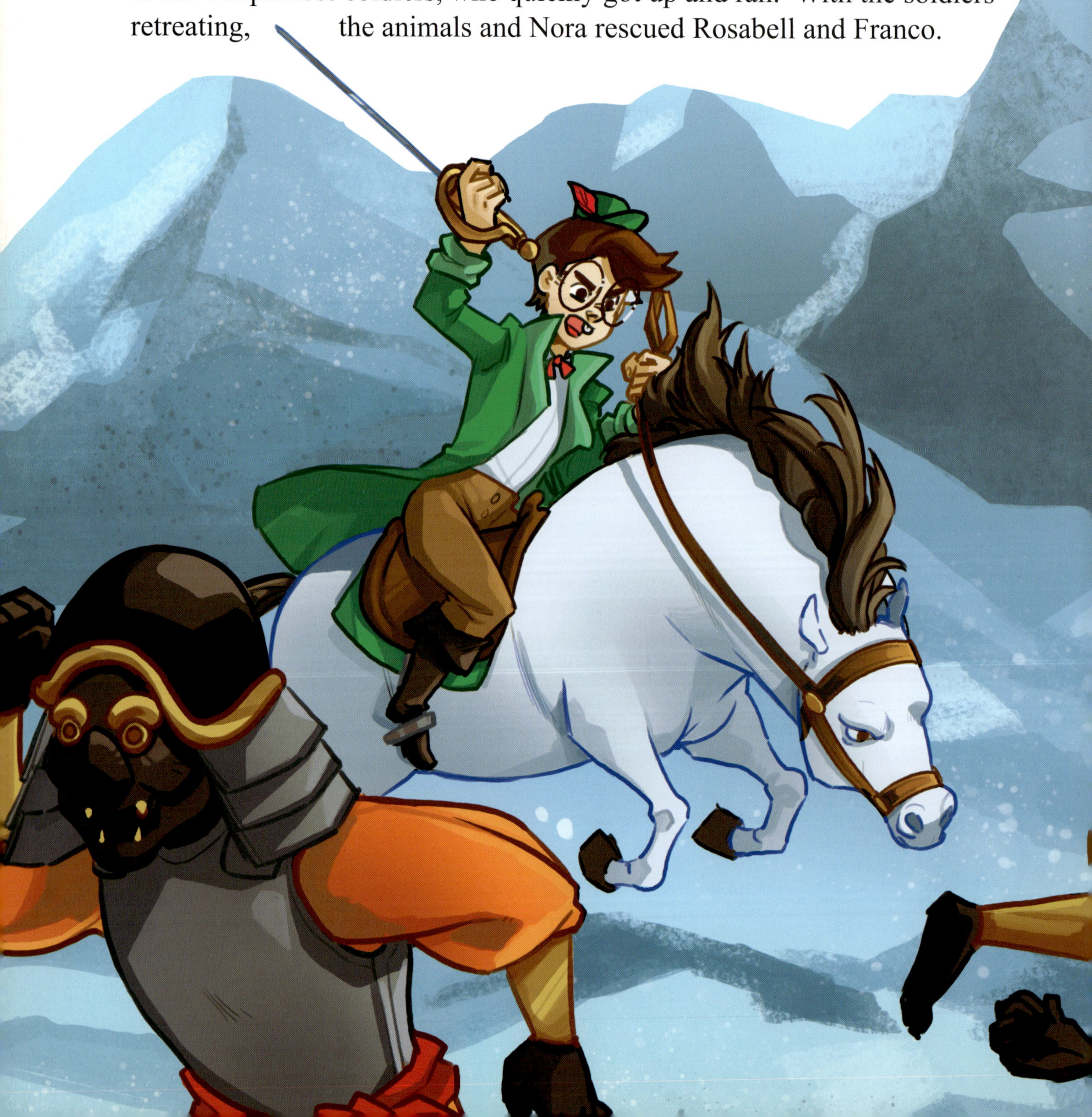

Liborio saw his former love was now free and thought the soldiers were nothing but cowards. This enraged Liborio, who's stone heart now overcame him. He grew in size, and his body transformed into a monster made completely out of stone.

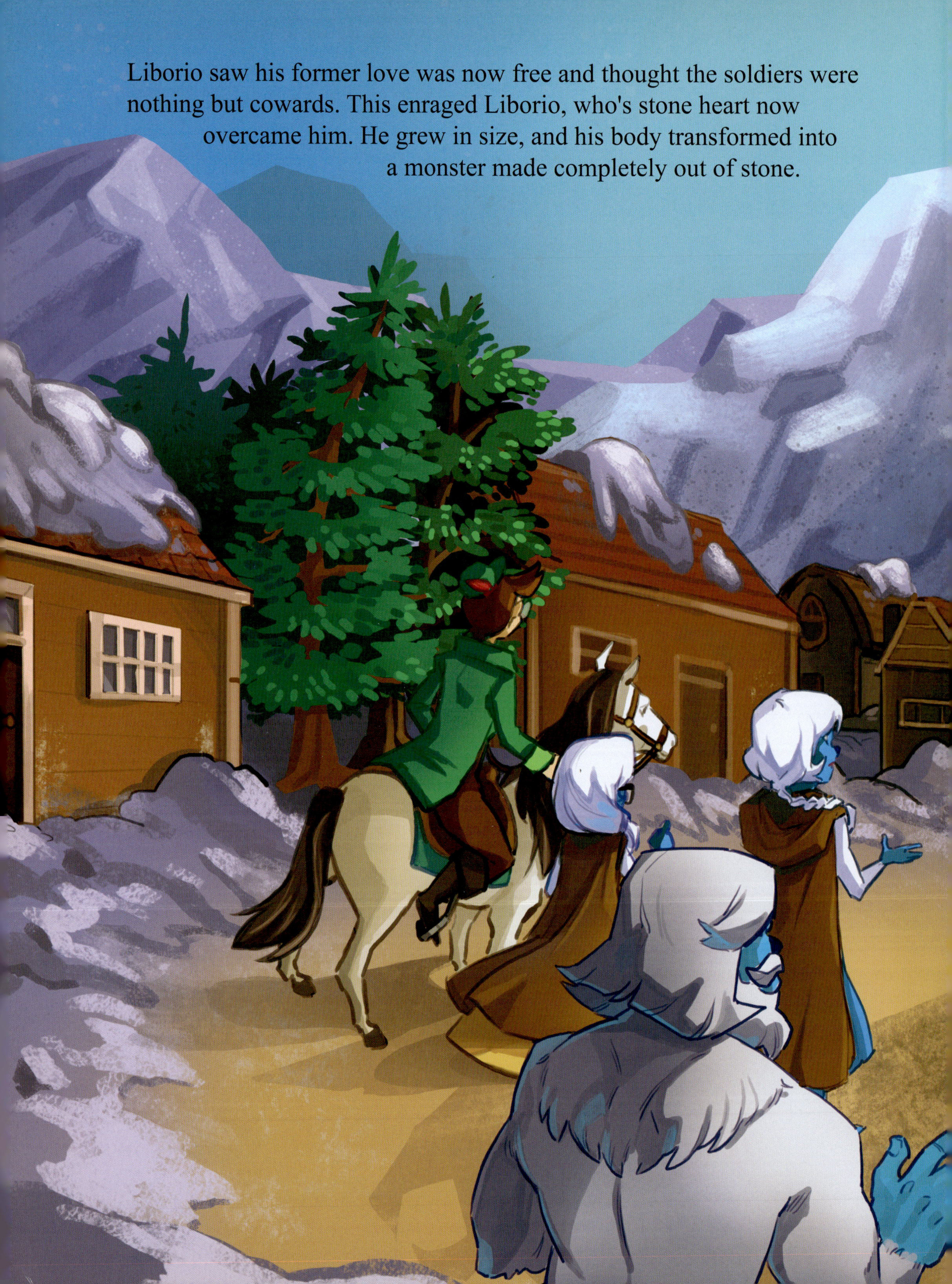

Liborio smashed his stone fists against the ground. They would all now pay for the betrayal of his one true love! Rosabell stood in front of everyone and told Liborio to stop. Liborio exclaimed,"Never!"

He raised his stone fists into the air to smash Rosabell. Orso suddenly appeared and stepped in the way of Liborio's massive stone fist, putting his paws up to stop the fist from crashing down on Rosabell.

He yelled,"Son! Stop this madness at once!" Liborio stunned from the voice, quickly pulled his fist away. His eyes gazed into Orso's and he transformed back into his human self. "Father?" The great bear Orso was the long lost wizard of Zermatt Castle.

Orso explained that he was hiking on the mountain and got caught in a terrible blizzard. He knew the only way he could save himself was to transform into a bear and hide in the caves of the mountain and hibernate until the storm passed. When he came out of hibernation, he couldn't remember how to transform back into his human self.

Rosabell and Franco were reunited with Nora and they embraced. Seeing this affection and being reunited with his father caused Liborio to feel shame for what he had done over all these years. Orso looked to the reunited family and exclaimed that Liborio must remove the curse he placed on Rosabell and Franco. But alas, Liborio could not. There was only one thing that could break the curse.

When Marco saw the love between Nora and her parents, he knew he felt that same love for Nora. She was a friend unlike any he had ever had. No one had ever done anything for him in the past without knowing his royal status. Nora turned from her parents to thank Marco for helping them.

Marco told Nora that she meant the world to him and would be his friend until the end of time. It didn't matter what she looked like because what was inside her was truly the most beautiful thing he'd ever seen. Marco hugged Nora with love in his heart. Suddenly the sky opened and beams of bright sun light shined down on Nora. Light and snow swirled around her.

Nora was transformed into a human girl. Now Marco was face to face with Princess Nora. They both gazed at each other with a loving innocent smile that neither of them had ever known. They hugged, then pulled back and looked deep into each other's eyes. The curse was broken.

The light beamed down on Rosabell and Franco, the snow swirled around them, and they were transformed into the noble king and queen that they rightfully were. Rosabell saw the sadness in Liborio's face as he knew what he had done over the years was wrong. She gave him a hug and forgave him.

Orso thanked Rosabell for her kindness and put his paws around Liborio. Hans looked at King Aldo with a smile, and Aldo put his paw on Hans's shoulder. Their days of fighting were over. The sun now shined brightly over the entire kingdom. Flowers bloomed, birds chirped.

The kingdom would soon be restored to it's former glory under the new rule of Queen Rosabell and King Franco, with their daughter Princess Nora and her new friend Prince Marco.

And they all lived happily ever after.

The End.